It is a big football match. Lots of fans go to go to the match!

At the game ...

... fans muck about and have fun!

At the game fans yell …

but in a wig and top hat?! Wicked!

At the game, fans can be cool.

But not him! He attacks the fans and gets led off.

At the game, fans can get hot in the sun ...

Are you a football fan? Do you back a team?

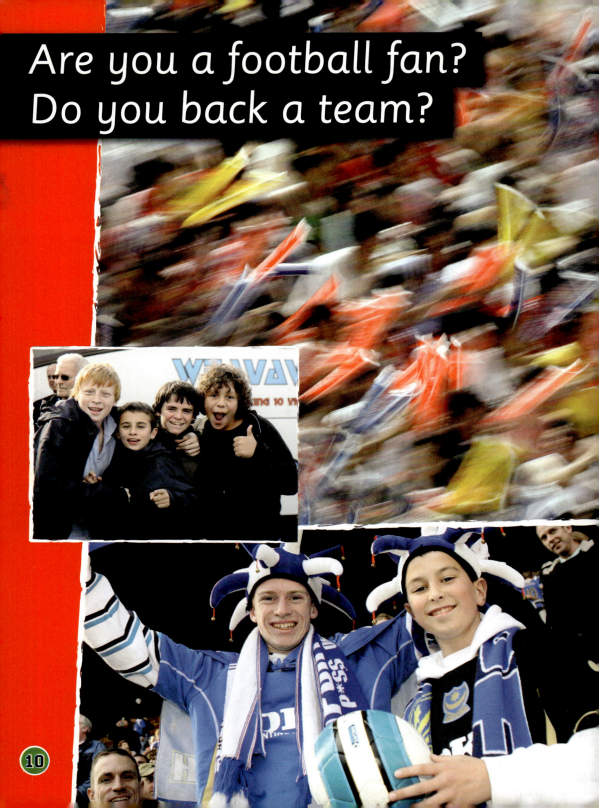